Toward Greater Peace and Security in Colombia

Forging a Constructive U.S. Policy

*Report of an Independent Task Force
Sponsored by the Council on Foreign Relations and
the Inter-American Dialogue*

Bob Graham and Brent Scowcroft, Co-Chairs
Michael Shifter, Project Director

The Council on Foreign Relations, Inc., a nonprofit, nonpartisan national organization founded in 1921, is dedicated to promoting understanding of international affairs through the free and civil exchange of ideas. The Council's members are dedicated to the belief that America's peace and prosperity are firmly linked to that of the world. From this flows the mission of the Council: to foster America's understanding of other nations, peoples, cultures, histories, hopes, quarrels, and ambitions and thus to serve our nation through study and debate, private and public.

THE COUNCIL TAKES NO INSTITUTIONAL POSITION ON POLICY ISSUES AND HAS NO AFFILIATION WITH THE U.S. GOVERNMENT. ALL STATEMENTS OF FACT AND EXPRESSIONS OF OPINION CONTAINED IN ALL ITS PUBLICATIONS ARE THE SOLE RESPONSIBILITY OF THE AUTHOR OR AUTHORS.

The Council will sponsor an Independent Task Force when (1) an issue of current and critical importance to U.S. foreign policy arises, and (2) it seems that a group diverse in backgrounds and perspectives may, nonetheless, be able to reach a meaningful consensus on a policy through private and nonpartisan deliberations. Typically, a Task Force meets between two and five times over a brief period to ensure the relevance of its work.

Given the timely nature of the policy issue, an interim report is produced to communicate the progress of the group's deliberations and recommendations. Upon reaching a final conclusion, the Task Force issues a complete report, and the Council publishes its text and posts it on the Council website. Task Force Reports can take three forms: (1) a strong and meaningful policy consensus, with Task Force members endorsing the general policy thrust and judgments reached by the group, though not necessarily every finding and recommendation; (2) a report stating the various policy positions, each as sharply and fairly as possible; or (3) a "Chairman's Report," where Task Force members who agree with the Chairman's Report may associate themselves with it, while those who disagree may submit dissenting statements. Upon reaching a conclusion, a Task Force may also ask individuals who were not members of the Task Force to associate themselves with the Task Force Report to enhance its impact. All Task Force Reports "benchmark" their findings against current administration policy in order to make explicit areas of agreement and disagreement. The Task Force is solely responsible for its report. The Council takes no institutional position.

For further information about the Council or this Task Force, please write the Council on Foreign Relations, 58 East 68th Street, New York, NY 10021, or call the Director of Communications at (212) 434-9400. Visit our website at www.cfr.org.

CONTENTS

[v]

FOREWORD

The Council on Foreign Relations and the Inter-American Dialogue were delighted to sponsor this important effort. Colombia, Latin America's third most populous country, has been suffering a long-term, persistent deterioration on many fronts. The implications for the United States and other countries in the hemisphere are significant. With the United States debating a major security assistance package, which has since been approved, we thought it would be useful to assemble a diverse group of U.S. policy and opinion leaders to examine Colombia's underlying problems, review U.S. policy toward that country, and develop recommendations for improving the policy. In 1998—even before the approval of the aid package—Colombia was already the third major recipient of U.S. security assistance in the world. It seemed clear that the country would, over time, occupy an even more prominent place on the U.S. foreign policy agenda.

Together, we launched an Independent Task Force on Colombia in November 1999. We were pleased that two of this country's most thoughtful public officials, Senator Bob Graham from Florida and former national security adviser General Brent Scowcroft, agreed to serve as co-chairs. We recruited Michael Shifter, a senior fellow at the Dialogue and an expert on Colombia, to direct the project. All three, in our view, have made a major contribution toward developing a coherent and comprehensive strategy toward Colombia.

In addition to putting together a distinguished group of Task Force members, we added a special and important feature to this effort by inviting a group of equally distinguished and diverse Colombians to serve as advisers (listed on page 39); their comments and input were very valuable. The Council and the Dialogue wish to thank all of these individuals for their outstanding contributions to this project.

The Task Force members met on three occasions, in December 1999 and in January and March of 2000. The discussions were animated and productive. At the end of March 2000, in response to the opportunity presented by congressional consideration of the aid package to Colombia, the Task Force produced an interim report, "First Steps Toward a Constructive U.S. Policy in Colombia," which was released by Senator Graham and General Scowcroft at a press briefing on Capitol Hill.

In the present report, the Task Force attempts to take a longer-term view. The report sets out broad parameters for a sustained and constructive U.S. strategy toward Colombia, taking into full account the country's massive problems and moving beyond the current emphasis on the drug problem. It argues that Colombia is experiencing pervasive lawlessness, insecurity, and corruption; U.S. policy should respond to these conditions, and most importantly, seek to build greater peace and security in that country. As the report points out, drugs are but one piece of a larger, more complex puzzle that needs to be tackled on all fronts, including curbing demand and consumption of illegal drugs in the United States. U.S. policy must move beyond drugs and include military, political, and socioeconomic dimensions. The report also maintains that the United States should be pursuing a more multilateral approach with European and Latin American allies, with Canada and Japan, and with international institutions and fora.

The report is unambiguous that Colombia matters a great deal to the United States and that significant national interests are at stake. Colombia's spreading lawlessness and criminality are destructive to such U.S. central objectives as deepening democracy, protecting human rights, expanding economic partnership, and fighting drugs. The Task Force members are keenly aware that no matter how enlightened U.S.-Colombia policy is, progress depends mostly on the citizens and government of that troubled country.

As the report points out, the United States will need sustained, high-level, bipartisan leadership on the Colombia policy challenge for many years to come. Whatever one thinks of the current aid package, a longer-term perspective is vital. This report is intended to inform the continuing debate and discussion about

Foreword

Colombia in Washington and beyond, and to offer practical proposals on how the United States can best respond to that country's agony. We very much hope that it contributes to better U.S. decision-making and policy.

Peter Hakim
President
Inter-American Dialogue

Leslie H. Gelb
President
Council on Foreign Relations

ACKNOWLEDGMENTS

The Independent Task Force on Colombia has been a collective endeavor that reflects the contributions and hard work of many individuals.

First and foremost, I am indebted to the superb co-chairs, Senator Bob Graham and General Brent Scowcroft. Their dedication, guidance, wisdom, and unstinting support over the past eight months made my job much easier. Ambassador Tony Gillespie of the Forum for International Policy and a Task Force member, and Bob Filippone, foreign policy adviser to Senator Graham, greatly facilitated work with both chairs.

I am also indebted to the Task Force members and observers, who generously shared their ideas and experiences. They participated energetically in the three meetings that took place at the Inter-American Dialogue in Washington, D.C.—in December 1999 and in January and March 2000—and offered valuable suggestions and advice on many drafts. The report reflects the views of those who participated in the Task Force, except as indicated in additional or dissenting views.

This Task Force also benefited substantially from the counsel and input provided by a group of Colombian advisers. These individuals reviewed drafts of the report at various stages and participated in a number of meetings with me during several visits to Colombia. Their keen observations and insights greatly enriched the final product. I particularly appreciate their collaboration.

The Task Force itself reflected a productive institutional collaboration between the Council on Foreign Relations and the Inter-American Dialogue, the organization where I work. At the Council in New York, I am grateful to Les Gelb, the Council's president, for his support and acute comments to clarify points in various drafts; Mike Peters, senior vice president, for his general assistance in coordinating the Task Force; Ken Maxwell, the

Council's director of the Latin America program, especially for his help in convening the Task Force and Colombian advisers; Colonel Kim McKenzie, the Council's Air Force Fellow from 1999 to 2000, who served as deputy director of the Task Force and worked closely with me; and Parag Khanna, a Council program associate, for keeping the process on track. Special thanks are also due to Paula Dobriansky, the vice president and director of the Council's Washington office, for her cooperation and support. The effort further benefited from the perspectives provided by the Council's San Francisco–based Working Group on Colombia, headed by Task Force member Mathea Falco, who kindly invited me to share some thoughts with the group in January 2000.

At the Dialogue, I am particularly grateful to Peter Hakim, the president, for his steadfast support and unsparing, yet constructive, criticism of several drafts. Pete Vaky, senior fellow at the Dialogue and Task Force member—who previously served as political officer and U.S. ambassador to Colombia—was a wonderful mentor and source of inspiration throughout the process. I profited immeasurably from his profound understanding of Colombia and his abiding affection for its people. Also at the Dialogue, I am indebted to Alvaro Herrero, for his fine research assistance, and to Jennifer Burrell and, later, Victoria Wigodzky, for their exemplary professionalism and skillful management of this effort.

Michael Shifter
Project Director

EXECUTIVE SUMMARY

At the dawn of the 21st century, few countries in the world are as deeply troubled as Colombia. This Andean nation—the third most populous in Latin America—is experiencing crises on many fronts. But at the same time the country possesses hopeful elements—the product of a resourceful and resilient people—coupled with an opportunity to forge a more democratic, peaceful, just, and prosperous nation.

Colombia has the potential to pursue a positive path and improve the quality of its democratic governance. But there are less benign possibilities on the horizon as well. The country could continue on its current course marked by widespread violence, lawlessness, and insecurity—the utter lack of protection of its citizens. And while it is important to caution against alarmist prognoses, it would be irresponsible to overlook the possibility of an even more dire outcome: the virtual collapse of state authority, accompanied by escalating instability, the further spread of criminality, and humanitarian horror.

This report is guided by the premise that the task of reversing the deterioration and setting Colombia on a more positive course lies fundamentally with the Colombians. The direction the country pursues is ultimately their responsibility. They have borne the enormous costs of the country's decline—and they will enjoy the fruits of whatever progress it makes.

But this report is also motivated by the belief—shared by most Colombians—that external support is critical to help put the country on a more peaceful and productive course. Many actors—private, nongovernmental, and governmental—that have been constructively involved in Colombia for a number of years continue to have essential roles in such an effort.

The U.S. government has a particularly crucial role to play. The United States has long been engaged in Colombia, and it is hard to imagine that it will disengage in the foreseeable future. Key U.S.

- Support efforts to help Colombia work out a political solution to its internal conflict. This means, concretely, employing greater diplomatic and political resources to work intensively with relevant actors and institutions in Colombia and the international community to pursue a settlement. In whatever agreement is reached, the United States should insist on strict adherence to lawful conduct.

- Provide security assistance to the Colombian armed forces. Such a focus should go hand in hand with diplomatic efforts to find a political solution to the conflict; this action should contribute to the larger goal of achieving peace. This can best be accomplished through greater attention to professionalizing and training the military and national police—and less relative attention to acquiring hardware. Appropriate human rights conditions and monitoring mechanisms should be included to ensure that the military performs its legitimate function in response to all violent, lawless actors in Colombia.

- Devote greater effort to deal with the drug problem. The United States should concentrate even more than it has to date on curbing demand in the United States, while at the same time strengthening the role of U.S. law enforcement agencies to respond more effectively to the supply challenge. To minimize the effect of displacing the problem from one location to another, a broader, multilateral approach that emphasizes greater coordination, control, and preventive social and institutional measures among affected countries is critical.

- Support efforts at institutional reform in the nonsecurity area. The U.S. government should go beyond what is contained in the current aid package and provide longer-term assistance to enable Colombia to pursue wide-ranging reforms. There should be an emphasis on judicial reform and rule of law efforts aimed at strengthening human rights guarantees and reducing corruption. Humanitarian assistance and well-developed social and alternative development programs that address underlying inequities in such areas as education, health, and land tenure patterns should also get priority.

- Provide special advantages in the trade area. The U.S. government should take every possible step to ensure that Colombian products have greater access to U.S. markets. At a minimum, this would mean immediately extending the Andean Trade Preferences Act (ATPA), or expanding it so that its benefits are comparable to those provided in the Caribbean Basin Initiative (CBI). Such measures should be undertaken on a region-wide basis.

- Seek actively to mobilize support within the hemisphere to help Colombia bring its conflict to an end. The U.S. government should encourage promising, collective efforts within the United Nations and the Organization of American States (OAS). The United States should also give priority attention to mobilizing resources from international financial institutions, the European Union, and bilateral donors to move toward achieving the wide-ranging goals set out in Plan Colombia. The United States should engage multilaterally in responding to the policy challenge posed by Colombia, in all of its complexity.

TASK FORCE REPORT

WHAT IS THE NATURE OF THE PROBLEMS IN COLOMBIA?

Colombia is a troubled country, beset by crime, corruption, and violence. On average, 25,000 Colombians die each year from diverse acts of violence; the country's homicide rate is among the highest in the world. In addition, more than half of the world's kidnappings take place in Colombia, a country characterized by rampant lawlessness and insecurity.

The problem is highlighted and compounded by the fact that even more than a decade after the end of the Cold War, two of the hemisphere's oldest insurgencies remain highly active forces in Colombia. Both the Revolutionary Armed Forces of Colombia (FARC) and the National Liberation Army (ELN) have deep political roots, dating back to the 1960s. The rural-based FARC—the larger of the two with approximately 15,000 combatants—is very strong militarily and financially. The ELN's roughly 3,000–5,000 combatants are concentrated in the northeast, where Colombia's oil industry is located; the ELN derives much of its income through kidnapping and extortion. The two groups, which enjoy little popular support, have combined revenues of at least several hundred million dollars a year.

Colombia also has paramilitary groups that emerged in response to insurgent advances and the inability of the country's debilitated and demoralized security forces to deal effectively with the growing conflict. They, too, have been operating for several decades and are by all accounts in a strong military and financial position today. They are estimated to number between 5,000 and 7,000 combatants. These militias—the most powerful and recognized being the United Self-Defense Forces of Colombia (AUC)—have grown more sophisticated over the years since the army and landowners first organized them as self-defense units. They have taken the law into their own hands.

Also adding to the mix of violence in Colombia are drug traffickers, previously concentrated in large cartels, but now increasingly fractured and spread out, making them harder to control. Indeed, to a considerable degree, the growing strength and capacity of the FARC and the paramilitary forces over the past several years can be attributed to a flourishing illegal narcotics industry. The industry fuels and benefits the FARC and the paramilitary forces in complex, but important, ways. The data in Colombia point to rising production, especially of coca and poppy, high levels of trafficking, and, most recently, signs of increasing consumption. Colombia accounts for some 80 to 90 percent of all of the cocaine produced in the world and a growing share of the heroin.

There is little question that the FARC, ELN, and paramilitary forces have evolved significantly since their emergence decades ago. Specialists disagree, however, about the extent to which they are still mainly political actors—or whether they now behave more as criminal groups or drug mafias. The lines are often blurred and difficult to determine with certainty. There is probably a measure of truth in both characterizations. Moreover, the insurgents and paramilitaries are large and fractured forces; the motivations and objectives of their many smaller units, spread throughout the large country, vary widely. The weight of evidence seems to suggest that the guerrilla groups' criminal activities are devoted to furthering both their economic and their political interests. The paramilitary groups, also, are seeking to expand their power and become part of Colombia's political game.

While specialists may dispute some of the characteristics of Colombia's violent groups, all concur that the country's internal conflict has huge costs. The conflict has claimed more than 35,000 Colombian lives in the past decade. According to the United Nations, Colombia's 1.5 million internally displaced population is the third largest in the world, following Sudan and Angola. Human rights abuses are among the most extensive in the hemisphere. According to both governmental and nongovernmental reports, the bulk of the politically related killings have recently been committed by paramilitary forces; the rest are committed by the insurgent groups and the armed forces.

Although the military's share of reported abuses has been significantly declining, there are major questions about links between the paramilitary forces and the state's security forces. Reports from the United Nations, the U.S. State Department, and such nongovernmental groups as Human Rights Watch suggest that in some cases direct connections between the two have been established. At a minimum, state agents have often merely looked the other way when paramilitary forces have committed atrocities.

Colombia is also now experiencing severe economic problems, which has made it more difficult for the country to deal effectively with its other, more longstanding, and worsening, problems. In 1999, as a result of both external and internal factors, the economy contracted by more than 5 percent—the worst slump since the 1930s. Colombia's unemployment rate, more than 20 percent, is among the highest in Latin America. A partial explanation for Colombia's uncharacteristic recession can be found in the effect of the 1997 Asian financial crisis. The external shock affected Colombia's economy (as it did several other Latin American economies), underscoring the country's vulnerability to the international financial system and the need for more effective preventive measures.

Moreover, recent attempts at institutional, political reform have produced some unfortunate, unintended consequences that have worsened the country's economic picture. Colombia, long known in the Latin American context for its political decentralization, developed a new constitution in 1991 that, among many things, granted greater fiscal authority to municipal governments. The advances in local autonomy have, however, been accompanied by fiscal imbalances that have put considerable strain on the country's finances. This factor contributed to the country's economic downturn in the mid-1990s. Moreover, many Colombians increasingly recognize that the flourishing illegal narcotics industry has not only exacerbated the country's violence and insecurity, but has, over time, had a negative effect on its economy as well.

All of these tendencies together have aggravated what has been evident for some time: the decay and deterioration of the country's institutions. Rampant corruption is a serious problem, one that has fueled and deepened the various crises—and hampered efforts to resolve them. Corruption has damaged many of the country's key institutions, including political parties and the Congress, the judicial system, and the executive branch of government.

Against this disturbing backdrop of insecurity on several fronts, an increasing number of Colombians have left their country. In the past four years, some 800,000 Colombians have emigrated, many to the United States, others to Europe, Canada, and to other Latin American countries. For many Colombians, minimal conditions to conduct business and function without fear no longer exist in their country. There is growing evidence of a "brain drain," of the departure of valuable human resources, especially to the United States.

To be sure, many of Colombia's problems are not entirely new. The widespread violence, for example, has a long history in Colombia. But it is also incorrect to assume that Colombia's current problems are merely more of the same. It is hard, for example, to find precedents for the country's severe recession and growing emigration, at least since the 1930s. In fundamental respects, these new features reinforce more longstanding problems. And the vast penetration of the drug problem in Colombia—and the resulting increase in violence and corruption—has had palpably negative consequences.

It is also crucial to challenge the all-too-familiar attitude that, because many of these problems have long been around, they will probably always be around. Such a counsel of resignation—the conclusion that not much can be done about Colombia's problems—needs to be rejected. In this spirit, it is important to probe more deeply and to attempt to grasp why these problems in Colombia have come together as they have and why they are so acute.

Toward Greater Peace and Security in Colombia

Colombia's multiple problems derive from a weak state, one that has historically had little presence in much of the national territory. The violence, criminal activities, and severe human rights and humanitarian problems are to a great extent the product of a state that has not been capable of performing its most elementary functions—protecting its citizens and upholding the rule of law.

In fact, many in Colombia who have violated the law have escaped prosecution and have not been held accountable for their crimes. The country's extremely high rate of impunity stems from an unresponsive and corrupt justice system that has been in part cause, and in part consequence, of the cumulative effect of Colombia's multiple crises. To date, various attempts to correct and reverse such conditions have had limited success.

The country's basic social services and infrastructure have also suffered as the result of a poorly functioning and weak state. Indeed, in many of Colombia's rural areas the state has been largely absent. Its disappointing performance in addressing the country's key social and economic problems has helped give rise to considerable discontent and unrest. The country's skewed land tenure patterns have been disruptive, producing significant flows of internal refugees. Such acute conditions help account for the origins of Colombia's active insurgent groups.

Colombia's armed forces have been similarly unable to prevent the country's continuing downward spiral. While measures of the military's strength and capacity vary, specialists contend that the armed forces are poorly trained and organized and have long been excessively bureaucratized. They have never had the resources they need—equipment, intelligence, or training—to respond in a professional and sustained way to the insurgent and paramilitary forces.

To be sure, the Colombian state faces formidable tasks in dealing with such serious and wide-ranging problems, in the context of impressive geographic diversity and a vast and heterogeneous nation. Constructing a coherent and unified nation has, historically, been a difficult challenge. Still, in the past, Colombian leaders were able to confront moments of crisis and come up with viable arrangements for dealing with them.

Today, however, Colombia's traditional political establishment—chiefly its two main political parties, the Liberals and Conservatives—appears to be much less up to the task of responding effectively to a national crisis than it has been in past years. The country's elite groups had previously been sufficiently cohesive to deal with public demands and to try to reach some accommodation. But today such groups are increasingly fragmented, which has made a unified and constructive policy response that much more difficult. Such splits have compounded a more longstanding problem having to do with Colombia's restricted and exclusionary political system.

Against this backdrop, three points deserve to be underlined.

First, Colombia's core, underlying problem is one of state authority and the maintenance of public order. The critical problem is the capacity to govern, to perform key functions. Other problems, including human rights violations and drug production and trafficking, are manifestations of the authority crisis—and in turn exacerbate the conflict.

Second, an analysis of Colombia's problems—and the reasons behind them—suggests the importance of distinguishing carefully between the short-term and longer-term challenges facing the country. Colombia's policy agenda is wide-ranging and demands long-term solutions. Many problems need to be addressed. Some, however, are more urgent than others. The security and authority problem, for example, is essential and can be regarded as a precondition for addressing the country's formidable social agenda.

And finally, though Colombians have the principal responsibility for resolving their own problems, it is clear that they would benefit substantially from external resources and support. There is an imbalance between the levels of resources (chiefly from the illegal narcotics industry) in the hands of violent, illegitimate groups and in the hands of legitimate, civilian authorities. Such an imbalance can only be corrected by an infusion of resources that comes from outside Colombia. In addition, a comprehensive approach—one that embraces military, political, economic, and social elements—can best contribute to a durable and effective solution to the country's problems.

The election of Andrés Pastrana as Colombia's president in June 1998 was met with high expectations—in Colombia and abroad—that the country would soon be in a better position to stop the deterioration. A new administration filled with bold ideas responded to a moment of widely shared public frustration. There was, it seemed, reason for hope.

From the outset, President Pastrana has identified the achievement of peace as his highest priority. Even before taking office in August 1998, he launched a process to explore a negotiated settlement with the FARC. As president, he granted a demilitarized zone to the FARC in southern Colombia, the group's principal stronghold, in an effort to build trust with the country's most powerful insurgency. In May 1999, the Colombian government and the FARC agreed on a common agenda and framework for discussions. In early 2000, FARC and government representatives went to several European capitals to explore alternative economic models.

Pastrana has, in short, taken a number of steps designed to put an end to the country's decades-old conflict. Attempts to establish a framework for discussions with the ELN—including a demilitarized zone with international verification—have also been under way. An agreement with Colombia's armed groups would then presumably enable his government to focus on other national problems, including the narcotics question and economic difficulties.

In addition, several of President Pastrana's policy measures in the areas of political reform and human rights have sought to address the country's troubled situation. Some of the steps President Pastrana has taken concerning the counter-narcotics question (for example, the resumption of extradition) and his plans for military reform hold some promise as well. In the economic sphere, policymakers in the Pastrana administration have generally shown prudence and sound judgment in attempting to improve the country's outlook.

At the end of the first year of his administration, Pastrana outlined his main ideas for moving the country forward in Plan Colombia ("Plan for Peace, Prosperity, and Strengthening of the State"), a comprehensive framework developed and agreed to by the Clinton and Pastrana administrations in September 1999. Plan Colombia calls for an expenditure of $7.5 billion over a four-year period to pursue five broad goals: advance the peace process; strengthen the national economy; enhance the counter-drug strategy; promote justice system reform and protect human rights; and foster greater democratization and social development.

Prospects for changing course in Colombia can also be seen in the country's more mobilized civil society. Pastrana's efforts can only succeed with the backing of key sectors. A political solution to the country's internal conflict would, after all, be difficult to achieve without the active participation of business groups. On this score, there have been noteworthy developments, including the meeting of influential business leaders with FARC representatives. Respected figures in Colombia's Catholic Church have also become more actively involved in the effort to end the armed conflict. And over the past several years, various nation-wide movements have brought together millions of Colombians to protest against rampant violence and kidnapping.

Within the international community as well there has been growing awareness and concern about Colombia's decline. Some of the European countries, Japan, the United Nations, and the relevant international financial institutions have shown an interest in contributing to Plan Colombia. Nongovernmental groups in the United States and Europe have been similarly activated. There have been encouraging offers to assist Jan Egeland, the U.N. secretary-general's special adviser on Colombia appointed in December 1999, to coordinate international support for the country.

These promising steps should not, however, obscure the fact that the Pastrana administration's performance in regaining control and authority of the country—in pursuing its highest priority—has been largely disappointing. The peace effort has struggled every step of the way, yielding few, if any, tangible results. There are serious and well-founded questions about whether the FARC is prepared to negotiate in good faith. Typically, welcome gestures, such as a holiday truce, are followed by continued and cruel armed conflict.

There have also been profound doubts raised, in Colombia and abroad, about the clarity, coherence, and even wisdom of the government's peace strategy. In Colombia, there has been scant, and declining, public confidence and support for President Pastrana's efforts. For many, there is a perception that a great deal has been conceded to a FARC insurgency that controls the initiative in the peace effort—and the Colombian government has gained little in return. The Pastrana administration, under considerable strain on many fronts, has had difficulty building the kind of internal political consensus that is essential to make progress in reaching a settlement with the violent groups.

For the current Colombian administration and those that follow, it will be crucial to pursue an end to the armed conflict by regaining control and authority over the national territory. The government will, over the long term, need to focus on building greater legitimacy by performing functions that ordinary citizens demand and deserve. Serious reforms that translate into greater justice—with key institutions being accessible to all Colombians—are essential. Yet also prominent among government functions is simply providing citizens with basic protection and ensuring their security. Building a stronger and more effective military and police force would help level the playing field, changing the calculations of the insurgents and inducing them to negotiate in good faith. In the long run, it would contribute to greater security and peace in Colombia.

External involvement in Colombia will doubtless be very important. The chances that such involvement in Colombia by the United States and other countries would be successful are greatly enhanced in light of the country's longstanding assets and advantages. Colombia has been described as a paradox, with deleterious trends taking place alongside positive ones. Yet the country has a number of favorable attributes that offer some grounds for hope and optimism.

Perhaps most important, Colombia has an impressive record of civilian, constitutional government; democratic rule and practice are longstanding. Even under Colombia's current beleaguered circumstances, there is little talk about replacing elected government with military rule. The Colombian government has also enjoyed some success in previous negotiations with several guerrilla groups. In the 1980s, for example, the M-19 guerrilla movement reached a settlement with the government and was then incorporated into the political system.

Colombia's history is replete with noteworthy political reforms, including the country's 1991 constitution, which contained provisions for greater citizen participation and representation as well as expanded legal guarantees. In short, Colombia has demonstrated time and again its ability to bring about important reforms. This is not a matter of "nation-building," but rather an effort to strengthen declining institutions.

Equally impressive, Colombia had long been Latin America's best economic performer; it never had to renegotiate its debt, as every other major Latin American country did in the 1980s. Until 1999, it was (together with Chile) the only country in the region whose bonds carried an investment grade rating. Colombia has also been blessed with plentiful natural resources and ample and talented human capital. It is, in short, a country with abundant resources—political, economic, human, and natural—that has the potential to move ahead in a positive direction.

WHY SHOULD COLOMBIA MATTER TO THE UNITED STATES?

There are five ways that Colombia's deterioration affects significant national interests of the United States.

First, between 80 and 90 percent of the cocaine and roughly two-thirds of the heroin consumed in the United States are produced in Colombia. To be sure, the drug problem needs to be dealt with in all of its dimensions, both on the demand and on the supply sides. But it is hard to see how any progress can be made on the supply end unless the Colombian state regains greater authority and increased control over its territory, including the ability to enforce its laws effectively and comprehensively. This change is crucial to help make Colombia a more effective partner with the United States in the common effort to deal with the drug problem.

Second, Colombia's deterioration spreads instability and conflict beyond its borders. Insurgent and paramilitary groups have made frequent incursions into the neighboring countries of Venezuela, Ecuador, and Panama. Such incursions could well increase. The wider region is increasingly uncertain, reflecting both real spillover effects and independent, troublesome political developments. A stronger Colombia means a stronger region and a stronger Western Hemisphere.

Third, there is potential for further deterioration of human rights and democracy in Colombia. The underpinnings of human rights protections and democratic institutions that have already eroded may move closer to collapse. Colombia's democratic future is at risk. A setback for democracy in Colombia would be a serious reversal for the region as a whole. It would undermine the important U.S. objective of building a secure, democratic, and prosperous hemispheric community.

Fourth, Colombia is an important economic partner for the United States. It is South America's fourth-largest economy and the fifth-largest U.S. export market in Latin America. An economically dynamic Colombia is a good customer, trading partner, and attractive opportunity for investment. Colombia's richness in natural resources offers great economic potential for the United States, especially in the oil and gas sectors. Greater U.S. economic engagement can also help Colombia strengthen and sustain the basis of its legal economy.

Finally, Colombia has the potential to become a more significant source of immigration into the United States. The influx of Colombians already coming to the United States—the numbers would doubtless go up if the situation were to deteriorate—is a sound reason why this Andean country matters to the United States.

Should current trends continue, and especially if economic circumstances take a turn for the worse in the United States, Colombian immigration would begin to impose growing strain on the capacity of affected state and city governments. The status of Colombians in the United States has already become an issue on the policy agenda and may become even more so.

For all of the above reasons, Colombia matters to the United States. The grave situation seriously affects U.S. national interests and poses an important policy challenge. This alone, however, is not sufficient to argue that the United States should in fact assist Colombia in a substantial way.

High-level U.S. engagement and support are called for because they are essential to begin to reverse the deterioration in Colombia. Moreover, other countries and institutions are likely to take their lead from the United States—and would be less inclined to commit significant resources without major U.S. involvement. The United States, perhaps alone among international actors, has the capacity to make a difference in Colombia.

Constructive U.S. support for Colombia would contribute to the overarching objectives that the United States is pursuing, and needs to pursue even more vigorously, in Latin America. The United States does, after all, have a major interest in trying to shape and build a hemispheric community that is democratic, stable, equitable, and prosperous. Too often, however, the United States tends to neglect problems in this hemisphere until they acquire the dimensions of a major crisis. In this case, the United States and Colombia have already waited too long to recognize and address their common problems directly and responsibly, including the consumption and production of illegal narcotics. It is time for the United States to attempt to deal more vigorously and cooperatively with an urgent agenda that greatly affects both countries.

The United States should also respond positively and in a sustained way to Plan Colombia, which was, after all, put together at the behest and urging of the Clinton administration. It would be irresponsible for the U.S. government to turn away from a plan that it had a major hand in devising. This is especially so because the plan represents a good, preliminary framework for dealing with Colombia's major problems. Although Plan Colombia is perhaps more a catalogue of problems than a coherent strategy for action, it nonetheless succeeds in setting out broad goals, making it clear that the Colombian government understands the multiple problems it faces. It also expresses a strong commitment to deal with the problems in a sensible and forceful way.

To be sure, growing involvement in Colombia carries some risk. But that risk can, as outlined below, be held in check. In the end, the risk is acceptable and worth taking, especially when weighed against the potential gain in terms of helping Colombia reverse its deterioration and pursue a more productive course.

A lack of constructive involvement in Colombia is likely to present even greater risks. In light of current dynamics in the country, there is ample reason to be concerned. Leaving the security question unattended in the short term—and the wider social, economic, and institutional agenda in the longer term—could very well produce the least desirable outcome for Colombia and for the United States. Indeed, without such engagement it would be reasonable to expect even further deterioration in the country's multiple crises, including its already critical human rights and humanitarian conditions.

WHAT ARE THE CHALLENGES AND GUIDELINES FOR U.S. POLICY?

Throughout much of the twentieth century, the United States and Colombia enjoyed close and friendly relations. This was due in some measure to Colombia's exemplary economic management and its traditional adherence to civilian, constitutional government since the late 1950s. For many years, Washington held up Latin America's third-largest country as a model of good governance and a close partner in President John F. Kennedy's Alliance for Progress aid program.

The relationship between the United States and Colombia has evolved substantially over the past several decades. In 1998, Colombia became the third largest recipient of U.S. security assistance in the world, following Israel and Egypt. The total amount of aid was $289 million, all for counter-narcotics efforts. In June 2000, in response to Plan Colombia, the U.S. Congress approved a significant increase in U.S. assistance, totaling some $1.3 billion over a two-year period. The proposal focuses on military assistance, aimed chiefly at the counter-narcotics effort. Support for alternative development, judicial reform, and rule of law activities is part of the package as well.

The principal, overall challenge for U.S. policy in Colombia is to fashion a broader, strategic, longer-term concept toward that country. The package approved in 2000 should be seen, at best, as a first step in a more sustained, engaged, bipartisan effort. In looking ahead, it is important to bear in mind two central considerations. First, the complexity of the gamut of issues posed by Colombia demands a comprehensive framework. To be most effective, the policy response should include military, economic, political, diplomatic, and social elements. These are necessarily mutually reinforcing.

Second, it is essential for U.S. policy to overcome a short-term horizon and be prepared for a longer-term involvement in Colombia. There is no quick fix, or one-shot approach, that will have any lasting, positive effect on Colombia. This does not mean that the United States will get dragged into a quagmire. On the contrary, with a clear focus on a balanced, wide-ranging approach the United States should develop the safeguards to avoid a slippery slope and identify a clearer exit strategy. Appropriate external assistance for perhaps a half dozen years would, realistically, help enable the Colombians to deal more effectively with their own problems. It is important, moreover, to be clear about such a commitment—and to communicate the message to the American public.

A longer-term, constructive U.S. policy should also be guided by the following considerations concerning five key challenges: drugs, conflict resolution, military and human rights questions, the U.S.-Colombia bilateral relationship, and a multilateral approach.

Drugs

Since the late 1970s, the drug question has dominated the relationship between Colombia and the United States. It is clear that both countries have a serious drug problem and that they have a shared responsibility to deal with it on all fronts, with even greater vigor than before. Much more can and should be done, including greater efforts aimed at education, treatment, and prevention programs in the United States. There also needs to be increased support for multilateral initiatives to monitor and address the drug problem. Such initiatives are particularly important in light of the balloon effect, which means that any attempt to reduce or control drug production in one place is likely to appear and pop up in another. The overall U.S. drug policy merits a careful reassessment to determine the most productive ways to limit and control the negative impact of illegal narcotics. To be sure, law enforcement efforts to address the drug problem also need to be fortified and given additional resources. In short, more vigorous policies need to be undertaken on all fronts.

The United States should not, however, have any illusions that it can solve its own drug problem through its policy toward Colombia. The U.S. government is setting itself up for failure if it defines this as the main goal of U.S. policy in Colombia. At the same time, the drug question, as previously discussed, is a crucial dimension that tends to exacerbate Colombia's multiple crises. It needs to be dealt with effectively to help reverse Colombia's deterioration—not to solve the drug problem in the United States. The emphasis needs to be on both demand and supply; these are not mutually exclusive, but rather strengthen one another.

Conflict Resolution

It is crucial for the U.S. government to find ways to contribute more effectively to greater social peace and reconciliation in Colombia. While U.S. policymakers prefer to focus on the drug question in dealing with Colombia, it is important to have this broader objective in mind. To be sure, the country's violent actors—the insurgent and paramilitary forces—are to a great extent inextricably intertwined with Colombia's substantial and pervasive drug economy. (While it may be possible to disentangle these actors from the narcotics question in theory, it is impossible to do so in practice.) However, the fundamental, core problem—the one that has to be addressed in order to make progress toward greater peace—has to do with state authority and security, the capacity of the government to protect its citizens. Strengthening this capacity would better enable the government to exercise its legitimate functions. It would be the best way to contain such violent actors as the insurgents and paramilitary groups, resolve the country's decades-old conflict, and thereby more effectively address the drug problem.

Military and Human Rights
The challenge for U.S. policy is how best to help Colombia improve its capacity to deal with the problems that are generating such widespread insecurity. The goals should be both effectiveness and strict adherence to human rights norms; these objectives reinforce one another. While focusing on military hardware and tactics may have some short-term benefits, the fundamental objective should be on attempting to professionalize the Colombian armed forces and police. This is the highest priority and would be the best use of resources. It puts more emphasis on training efforts, intelligence-gathering activities, and the like. It necessarily involves a long-term effort. And it would signal that pursuing the security question does not necessarily involve such a significant emphasis on drugs.

The Colombian military has been problematic; it has had a history of human rights violations and links with paramilitary forces. One view reflects deep concern about the possibility of U.S. military assistance tarnishing the United States through its association with a military credibly charged with human rights violations. Another view, however, would underscore the opportunity for the United States to gain greater leverage with the Colombian military, consistent with the norms that are part and parcel of a professionalization effort. Such an approach would emphasize the importance of trying to build a military capability that would be committed to responding to violence, whatever the source, within a context of respect for human rights. This would carry impor-

effective assistance programs to such key countries as Peru, Bolivia, and Ecuador, and closely coordinating efforts with Venezuela, Panama, and Brazil.

- *Political and Diplomatic:* It is important to support Colombia's effort to bring the conflict to an end. Structures need to be developed and put in place to accomplish constructive objectives. There are two priority areas: first, Colombia's hemispheric neighbors (Peru, Venezuela, Ecuador, Panama, and Brazil), all of which are affected by Colombia's deterioration; and, second, the European countries, Canada, and Japan, all of which are increasingly concerned about Colombia and the wider, regional implications. The U.S. government can and should play a positive role in mobilizing support among these governments. It should also, when appropriate, encourage and assist efforts undertaken either by the OAS or the United Nations. The U.N. secretary-general's special adviser assigned to Colombia, Jan Egeland, deserves full support and an expanded mandate.

- *Economic and Financial:* The United States needs to welcome and press for multilateral assistance on the economic and financial fronts as well. This is critical to provide adequate support for pieces of Plan Colombia that are not covered by the United States but are essential to the plan's success. In this effort, the contributions of the European Union, the Andean Development Corporation, and the international financial institutions—the International Monetary Fund, the World Bank, and the Inter-American Development Bank—are vital.

ADDITIONAL VIEWS

I support the report and applaud Senator Graham and General Scowcroft for taking on this important responsibility. I would offer three comments. First, the history of paramilitary violence against former guerrillas who entered the democratic process requires that the paramilitaries be disarmed as part of any peace settlement. Second, President Pastrana inherited a Colombian state and economy severely weakened by the previous Samper administration and the sanctions imposed on Colombia due to Samper's corruption. While President Pastrana has made mistakes, his administration deserves high marks for launching the peace process and reviving the economy. Third, the peace process in Colombia requires for success the same kind of sustained, high-level international involvement and support as the peace processes in Central America, Northern Ireland, and the Middle East.

Bernard Aronson

I agree with the thrust of the well-reasoned majority report by the Independent Task Force on Colombia. Accordingly, I concur with the vast majority of its findings and recommendations. These concurring views are offered to provide context and additional facts.

Although the report accurately describes a deteriorating security situation in Colombia, as well as the need for special attention to human rights and Colombia's own obligations in restoring stability, I believe it is missing context. Specifically, why is Colombia suddenly so important, particularly if the level of violence in Colombia has been historically high and the guerrilla groups date back to the 1960s? Why did the administration begin intensely focusing on Colombia over the past year and a half? And why should the average American—or member of Congress or incoming president—care at all (much less, deeply) about the state of affairs in Colombia?

Central to the entire discussion of Colombia is the impact of illegal drugs. The reason Colombia has surged onto the political and military, human rights, and world financial agenda is that, over the past five years, Colombia has become the world's number one producer, processor, and exporter of cocaine, a deadly and illegal narcotic. While the Task Force Report acknowledges that drugs are "a problem," one is left with the sense that drug trafficking profits-cum-violence are just one of many equally important contributors to the mounting instability. I believe that drugs are the leading cause, not merely one of many co-equal causes. I think it is not inaccurate to say that the inability of Colombia's honest and committed presidential leadership to achieve results in the peace process, and otherwise stabilize the country politically and economically, is the result of a python-like stranglehold by the Colombian drug traffickers on the overall process.

To be specific, lasting peace requires that the guerrillas give up their drug funding and well-documented trafficker ties—a connection that reportedly generates between 60 and 100 million dollars in drug money for them per month—or they cannot be understood to be negotiating in good faith. The insurgent groups are composed of both common (or war) criminals who have murdered hundreds of innocent people and receive their funding from the increasingly wealthy drug traffickers and genuine aspirants for legitimate political involvement. Until the latter group separates itself from the former and clearly forswears involvement in the drug trade, there can be no such thing as good faith negotiation for peace. Without this condition being met, drugs will continue to taint the peace process and justify Colombia's use of U.S. counter-drug aid against all those allied with drug trafficking.

The United States must maintain—for our own national security, regional security, and Colombia's stability—a commitment to strengthening direct support for those in Colombia openly arrayed against the traffickers and narcotics-funded guerrillas, including the judiciary, prosecutors, law enforcement (especially the Colombian National Police), and military. While human rights must always be respected, peace will only come when Colombia can negotiate from a position of strength.

Colombia is not El Salvador, Nicaragua, Vietnam, or Somalia. As the Task Force Report carefully explains, Colombia is a nation with a history of respected democratic institutions, international trade, sound and reliable economic institutions and industries, a respect for human life, community, family, and human rights, with a potentially bright future. What has caused Colombia to begin radiating violence and instability from its critical position in the hemisphere—resulting in deaths of more than 10,000 young Americans due to use of imported cocaine and heroin, and drug-funded terrorism on a larger scale in Colombia than ever before—is the elevation of drugs. While there is a crying need for more drug prevention and for expanded substance abuse treatment, the security of America's youth will continue to depend, ironically, on how we respond to the threat in Colombia.

To a large extent, the consensus that emerged in late 1999, which should animate policymakers, stems from factors not otherwise discussed in the report, namely:

- A growing realization that Peru and Bolivia are succeeding in knocking out major coca growing regions for the first time in decades;

- A growing realization that Colombia is the source of most of the cocaine and heroin arriving in the United States;

- A growing realization that drug prevention and treatment efforts in the United States, while vitally important, cannot alone overcome the widening impact of imported illegal drugs, especially cocaine and heroin;

- A realization that Colombia's honest government cannot bring the narcotics-funded guerrillas to the negotiating table for peace unless they can demonstrate that they have the ability to negotiate from strength;

- A realization among most observers that Colombia's honest government cannot gain a position of strength in these negotiations without the help of the United States;

- A realization among most observers that this help must be sustained, consistent, comprehensive, and include military and law enforcement support and assets; and

- A realization that current decisions are inextricably bound by context, especially Colombia's role in the drug trade.

Robert Charles

Although I agree with much of the substance of the report, I have serious reservations about the following points.

The two-year $1.3 billion U.S. aid package concentrates largely on providing military equipment to Colombia. The Task Force Report assumes that this is the first step in a much longer, more comprehensive U.S. assistance program for Colombia, which the report argues is necessary to address Colombia's many internal problems. Although I agree that Colombia needs substantial help, the current focus on military assistance will most probably make the possibility of sustained, high-level U.S. aid unlikely. Giving the Colombian military advanced helicopters and other security equipment to combat narcoterrorists will cause the guerrillas to multiply their armed attacks and increase the sophistication of their weaponry, which they can well afford to do. This escalation of the conflict will reduce the chances that there will be political support in the United States for providing assistance to Colombia over the longer term.

The administration and the Congress are kidding themselves if they believe that this aid package will achieve its stated objectives, namely, to reduce substantially illicit drug production in Colombia and to curtail the flow of drugs to the United States. Strong demand for cocaine and heroin in the United States will continue to fuel the drug traffic. Even if the Colombians succeeded in destroying a substantial portion of their drug crops, which even their own leaders do not think will happen anytime soon, Americans would have little trouble finding drugs from other sources, including Colombia's neighbors, Brazil and Venezuela, where drug production is already expanding. As long as millions of Americans are willing to pay for drugs, there will be no shortage of suppliers.

The U.S. aid package relies too heavily on high-tech equipment, particularly Black Hawk helicopters, which the Colombians acknowledge they will have trouble operating and maintaining without U.S. help. This will require significant numbers of U.S. technical personnel who are likely to become targets of reprisals from the guerrilla groups. As attacks multiply against U.S. personnel, the United States will be faced with unsatisfactory choices: either increase the presence of armed American military or withdraw the advisers.

The Task Force Report overlooks a real opportunity for the United States to undertake an active mediating role in Colombia. The multilateral diplomatic efforts endorsed by the report are unlikely to produce results. However, a strong U.S. diplomatic role could bring the government and the various guerrilla factions to the negotiating table. The FARC's responsibility for the recent murder of three Americans should not prevent the United States from asserting leadership, if, as I am convinced, it is in the U.S. national interest to help bring an end to the current crisis in Colombia by diplomatic means.

Mathea Falco

I fully endorse the report. With respect to performance criteria and benchmarks, though, I believe that there are three important points to bear in mind. First, any such benchmarks must be set and applied in a flexible manner. The Colombian crisis is highly fluid and, regrettably, will continue to exist for some time. Conditions will be changing, and during the process one can expect serious setbacks. It is important that U.S. assistance to Colombia not be readily derailed by such developments. Second, in designing and implementing conditions and measuring criteria, policymakers shoud resist the temptation to draw distinctions between anti-narcotic and anti-insurgent activities. As the report suggests, at least for many knowledgeable observers, the line between criminal, as opposed to insurgent, activity of the antistate forces is thoroughly blurred. It is not practical to combat the one without combating the other, and the conditions on international assistance should not force the Colombian government into

that extend beyond traditional security concerns, that is likely to be at the top of our list of foreign policy concerns.

Finally, we must recognize that the balloon-effect problem noted in the report is inextricably linked to our own failure to deal with the drug problem in the United States. We pushed some of the drug barons out of Colombia's neighbors. And they resurfaced in Colombia. We helped defeat the big cartels, and they were replaced by smaller, more flexible mini-cartels. So long as there is huge drug demand in the United States, we will always have Colombias. Unfortunately for us, in the future, they may not be so far away or remote from the thoughts of so many Americans. Already, our neighbors in the Caribbean and especially in Mexico have been corrupted and rocked by the business of transshipping Colombian cocaine and heroin. Failure to deal with Colombia now poses the threat that the story of the first part of this new century will not be the optimistic tale of the spread of democracy that dominated speeches at the Summit of the Americas in 1994. Rather, it will be the story of the spread of a corrupting force that will in fact undermine democracy, tear at societies, play at the growing divisions between rich and poor in the hemisphere, and leave a generation asking, "Why did we fail to address this problem earlier?"

Consequently, while endorsing the report wholeheartedly, I seek to amplify the urgency of many of its points and to underscore those that are stated in language that is somewhat more measured and diplomatic. Containing the problem will require restoring peace. Restoring peace will mean the Colombian government must clearly be in a position to win and to punish the rebels for continuing to fight. Supporting the Colombian government in this will require that we deal with thorny problems such as political corruption and human rights violations in the best way possible without running away from them. And winning in Colombia is itself only a short-term solution if we don't make real progress in the war against drugs at home.

David J. Rothkopf

DISSENTING VIEW

The Independent Task Force Report contains many valuable elements, particularly its call for a long-term, multifaceted, and multilateral approach to Colombia's multiple crises. We applaud its emphasis on the peace process, respect for human rights, and the shared responsibility of the United States and Colombia for the drug problem. Nonetheless, the report privileges Colombia's security and authority problems rather than the legitimacy crisis that is both cause and effect of weak democratic institutions. Colombia's crisis of legitimacy is rooted in a history of exclusionary politics, deep poverty, vast social inequalities, human rights abuse, and impunity, all of which have sapped public confidence in Colombia's political institutions. These are fundamentally political, not security problems.

Because of the primacy attached to security issues, the report emphasizes—inappropriately, in our view—bolstering the military capacity of the state as the key to resolving other crises. To the extent that the recuperation of the state's legitimacy has a military dimension, it rests on restoring the state's monopoly on the use of force in a democratic context. As the report states but does not sufficiently underscore, this can only be achieved by targeting paramilitary groups as vigorously as those of the insurgent left. President Pastrana has fired several high-ranking officers with ties to paramilitary groups. This is a courageous beginning to what must be a sustained effort to sever the armed forces' relationship with the paramilitaries and reorient Colombian security doctrine to treat all private armies as threats to democratic governance, regardless of their political orientation. Progress toward both these goals should be subject to independent verification by neutral observers. Without a severance of such ties and a fundamental shift in orientation, security assistance will not aid the peace process but rather contribute to its failure.

Toward Greater Peace and Security in Colombia

The Task Force Report argues that the expanded U.S. military assistance plan will give the United States more leverage to ensure that human rights are respected in Colombia and paramilitary forces are not permitted to operate with impunity. Yet as the Central American example demonstrates, leverage is only useful to the extent that it is exercised. In Colombia, the multiple goals of U.S. policy and the priority assigned to curbing the drug trade pose the danger that security and antidrug objectives will be pursued more vigorously than peace and human rights.

Finally, peace processes elsewhere in the world demonstrate that the decision to seek peace has political and psychological, as well as military dimensions. We therefore support the Task Force recommendation for a multilateral political and diplomatic initiative for a negotiated settlement, involving European and Latin American allies as well as international organizations, including the United Nations.

Cynthia Arnson
J. Samuel Fitch

TASK FORCE MEMBERS AND OBSERVERS

Chairs

BOB GRAHAM is in his third term as a member of the U. S. Senate (D-Fla.) and previously served as governor of Florida.

BRENT SCOWCROFT is president of the Forum for International Policy and former national security adviser to President Bush.

Members

ELLIOTT ABRAMS is president of the Ethics and Public Policy Center. Formerly, he was assistant secretary of state for inter-American affairs.

STANLEY S. ARKIN is a partner and distinguished civil rights lawyer at Arkin Kaplan & Cohen LLP.

CYNTHIA ARNSON is assistant director of the Latin American Program at the Woodrow Wilson International Center for Scholars.

BERNARD ARONSON is managing partner of ACON Investments LLC and served as assistant secretary of state for inter-American affairs.

JOYCE CHANG is managing director of emerging markets research at Chase Securities.

ROBERT CHARLES is president of Direct Impact LLC and former chief of staff for the U.S. House National Security Subcommittee.

MIKE DEWINE is a member of the U. S. Senate (R-Ohio). He serves on the Senate's Judiciary Committee, the Senate's Drug Caucus, and is a former member of the House International Relations Committee.

JORGE I. DOMÍNGUEZ is the Clarence Dillon Professor of International Relations and director of the Weatherhead Center for International Affairs at Harvard University.

MATHEA FALCO, a lawyer, is president of Drug Strategies, a nonprofit research institute in Washington, D.C. She served as assistant secretary of state for international narcotics matters and chairs this year's Council on Foreign Relations Working Group on Colombia based in San Francisco.

J. SAMUEL FITCH is a professor of political science at the University of Colorado at Boulder.

SERGIO J. GALVIS is a partner at Sullivan & Cromwell, where he coordinates the firm's Latin American practice.

MICHAEL GAVIN is executive director of economic and financial research for Latin America at Warburg Dillon Read.

CHARLES GILLESPIE is resident senior fellow at the Forum for International Policy. He is a former U.S. ambassador to Colombia.

RICHARD HAASS is vice president and director of the foreign policy studies program at the Brookings Institution. He was special assistant to President Bush and senior director for Near East and South Asian Affairs at the National Security Council.

HENRY ALLEN HOLMES is an adjunct professor at Georgetown University and former assistant secretary of defense.

JAMES JONES is chairman of the U.S. Council of the Mexico-U.S. Business Committee, counsel at Manatt, Phelps & Phillips, and former ambassador to Mexico.

GEORGE JOULWAN is a retired general and former commander-in-chief of the U.S. Southern Command.

Task Force Members and Observers

ANTHONY W. LAKE is distinguished professor of diplomacy in the School of Foreign Service at Georgetown University. Previously, he served as national security adviser to President Clinton.

ABRAHAM F. LOWENTHAL is president of the Pacific Council on International Policy at the University of Southern California. He was founding executive director of the Inter-American Dialogue and director of the Center for International Studies at the University of Southern California.

THOMAS F. MCLARTY III is vice chairman of Kissinger McLarty Associates and former White House chief of staff.

THOMAS MCNAMARA is president of the Americas Society and former U.S. ambassador to Colombia.

AMBLER H. MOSS JR. is director of the Dante B. Fascell North-South Center at the University of Miami. Previously, he served as U.S. ambassador to Panama.

LILIA L. RAMÍREZ is a retired naval officer and congressional relations director for Navy and Marine Corps programs at the Raytheon Corporation.

ERVIN J. ROKKE is president of Moravian College in Bethlehem, Pennsylvania, and a former career officer in the U.S. Air Force.

DAVID J. ROTHKOPF is chairman and CEO of the Intellibridge Corporation and adjunct professor of international affairs at Columbia University. Previously, he served as managing director of Kissinger Associates and as deputy under secretary of commerce for international trade policy.

KATHLEEN KENNEDY TOWNSEND is lieutenant governor of the State of Maryland. Previously, she was deputy assistant attorney general in the U.S. Department of Justice.

VIRON P. VAKY is senior fellow at the Inter-American Dialogue. Formerly, he was assistant secretary of state for inter-American affairs and U.S. ambassador to Colombia.

ALEXANDER F. WATSON is vice president and executive director of the international conservation program at the Nature Conservancy. Formerly, he was assistant secretary of state for inter-American affairs.

Observers

LEE CULLUM is a columnist for the *Dallas Morning News* and a regular commentator on "The NewsHour with Jim Lehrer."

KAREN DEYOUNG is assistant managing editor at *The Washington Post.*

COLOMBIAN ADVISERS

JORGE CÁRDENAS is chief executive officer of the National Federation of Coffee Growers of Colombia.

FERNANDO CEPEDA is a professor of political science at University of the Andes in Bogotá. Previously, he was Colombian minister of government and ambassador to the Organization of American States.

FRANCISCO JOSÉ DE ROUX is director of the Program of Development and Peace in the Magdalena Medio.

GUSTAVO GALLÓN is director of the Colombian Commission of Jurists.

ANA MERCEDES GÓMEZ is the director of the daily newspaper *El Colombiano*. She also serves as a member of the National Conciliation Commission and Mass Media for Peace.

CARLOS LLERAS is director of the daily newspaper *El Espectador*. Previously, he was a presidential candidate, Colombian ambassador to the United States, and a member of the National Constitutional Assembly.

JUAN LUIS LONDOÑO is director of Dinero Publications in Bogotá. Formerly, he served as minister of health under the Gaviria administration and worked at the Inter-American Development Bank in Washington, D.C.

GUILLERMO PERRY has been chief economist of the Latin America and Caribbean division at the World Bank and is currently working in the private sector in Colombia. Previously, he was minister of finance, as well as a member of the National Constitutional Assembly and the Senate.

GUSTAVO PETRO is a member of Colombia's House of Representatives. Formerly, he was a member of the M-19 and served as that group's peace negotiator during the Barco administration.

EDUARDO POSADA is senior lecturer in history at the University of London's Institute of Latin American Studies. He is a columnist at *El Tiempo* and previously was director of *Diario del Caribe*.

JUAN EMILIO POSADA is the president of ACES Airlines in Colombia. Previously, he worked as manager of precious metals with R.D. Shells's Billiton Marketing in the Netherlands, as vice president international at Banco Cafetero, Colombia, and as commercial assistant with Colcafe, Colombia.

AUGUSTO RAMÍREZ OCAMPO* is currently the minister of development. In the past, he has been a member of the National Conciliation Commission; he also served as minister of foreign relations and as mayor of Bogotá.

JORGE RAMÍREZ OCAMPO is chair of the Banco Sudameris and independent consultant in international trade and economic integration. Previously, he was minister for economic development, president of the National Exporters Association, and coordinator of the Americas Business Forum.

ALFREDO RANGEL is a military analyst and former national security adviser to President Samper. He currently teaches at the University of the Andes in Bogotá.

NICANOR RESTREPO is president of the Compañía Suramericana de Seguros. He was president of the Latin American Business Council (CEAL) and of the Corporación Financiera Suramericana.

PEDRO RUBIANO SÁENZ is the archbishop of Bogotá.

MARÍA ISABEL RUEDA is a member of Colombia's Congress.

JUAN SALCEDO LORA is a retired general from the Colombian army and former director of the Escuela Superior de Guerra.

JAVIER SANÍN is the dean of the department of political science and international relations at Javeriana University in Bogotá. He is director of the magazine *Revista Javeriana* and a columnist for *El Colombiano*. Previously, he served as a member of the Commission for the Reform of Colombia's Political Parties.

Colombian Advisers

JULIO MARIO SANTO DOMINGO is president of the board of directors of the Bavaria Grupo Santo Domingo.

JUAN MANUEL SANTOS* is currently the minister of finance. Previously, he was president of the Good Government Foundation in Bogotá, and before that he served as vice president and minister of trade.

ENRIQUE SANTOS CALDERÓN is director of the Colombian newspaper *El Tiempo*. For 25 years, he wrote the influential column "Contraescape," for which he received the National Award for Journalism on three occasions. He was also a member of the commission that negotiated with various guerrilla groups during the Betancur administration.

GABRIEL SILVA is former Colombian ambassador to the United States.

MIGUEL SILVA is president of Semana Publications in Bogotá. Formerly, he practiced international law at the New York–based firm Shepardson, Stern & Kaminsky, worked as chief of staff at the Organization of American States, and served as secretary general of the presidency under the Gaviria administration.

ENRIQUE UMAÑA is president of Coinvertir, a nonprofit organization established by the government and leading national and multinational companies to promote foreign investment in Colombia.

ALVARO URIBE VÉLEZ practices law in Medellín. Formerly, he served as senator in the Congress, as governor of Antioquia, and as mayor of Medellín.

ALVARO VALENCIA is a retired general from the Colombian army.

LUIS CARLOS VILLEGAS is president of the National Association of Industrialists (ANDI) and the European–Latin American Business Association. Previously, he served as senator, minister of foreign affairs, and governor of the Risaralda department.

---

*Served as adviser before assuming ministerial role.

OTHER REPORTS OF INDEPENDENT TASK FORCES
SPONSORED BY THE COUNCIL ON FOREIGN RELATIONS

*†*Promoting Sustainable Economies in the Balkans* (2000)
Steven Rattner, Chairman; Michael B.G. Froman, Project Director

*†*Nonlethal Technologies: Progress and Prospects* (1999)
Richard L. Garwin, Chairman; W. Montague Winfield, Project Director

*†*U.S. Policy Toward North Korea: Next Steps* (1999)
Morton I. Abramowitz and James T. Laney, Co-Chairs; Michael J. Green,
Project Director

†*Safegarding Prosperity in a Global System: The Future International Financial
Architecture* (1999)
Carla A. Hills and Peter G. Peterson, Co-Chairs; Morris Goldstein, Project
Director

*†*Strengthening Palestinian Public Institutions* (1999)
Michael Rocard, Chair; Henry Siegman, Project Director

*†*U.S. Policy Toward Northeastern Europe* (1999)
Zbigniew Brzezinski, Chairman; F. Stephen Larrabee, Project Director

*†*The Future of Transatlantic Relations* (1999)
Robert D. Blackwill, Chair and Project Director

*†*U.S.-Cuban Relations in the 21st Century* (1999)
Bernard W. Aronson and William D. Rogers, Co-Chairs; Walter Russell Mead,
Project Director

*†*After the Tests: U.S. Policy Toward India and Pakistan* (1998)
Richard N. Haas and Morton H. Halperin, Co-Chairs; Cosponsored by the
Brookings Institution

*†*Managing Change on the Korean Peninsula* (1998)
Morton I. Abramowitz and James T. Laney, Co-Chairs; Michael J. Green,
Project Director

*†*Promoting U.S. Economic Relations with Africa* (1998)
Peggy Dulany and Frank Savage, Co-Chairs; Salih Booker, Project Director

†*U.S. Middle East Policy and the Peace Process* (1997)
Henry Siegman, Project Director

†*Russia, Its Neighbors, and an Enlarging NATO* (1997)
Richard G. Lugar, Chair; Victoria Nuland, Project Director

*†*Differentiated Containment: U.S. Policy Toward Iran and Iraq* (1997)
Zbigniew Brzezinski and Brent Scowcroft, Co-Chairs; Richard Murphy, Project Director

Rethinking International Drug Control: New Directions for U.S. Policy (1997)
Mathea Falco, Chair and Project Director

*†*Financing America's Leadership: Protecting American Interests and Promoting
American Values* (1997)
Mickey Edwards and Stephen J. Solarz, Co-Chairs; Morton H. Halperin,
Lawrence J. Korb, and Richard M. Moose, Project Directors

†*A New U.S. Policy Toward India and Pakistan* (1997)
Richard N. Haass, Chair; Gideon Rose, Project Director

†*Arms Control and the U.S.-Russian Relationship: Problems, Prospects, and Pre-
scriptions* (1996)
Robert D. Blackwill, Chairman and Author; Keith W. Dayton, Project Director;
Cosponsored with the Nixon Center

†*American National Interests and the United Nations* (1996)
George Soros, Chair

*Available from Brookings Institution Press. To order, call 1-800-275-1447.
†Available on the Council on Foreign Relations website at www.cfr.org.